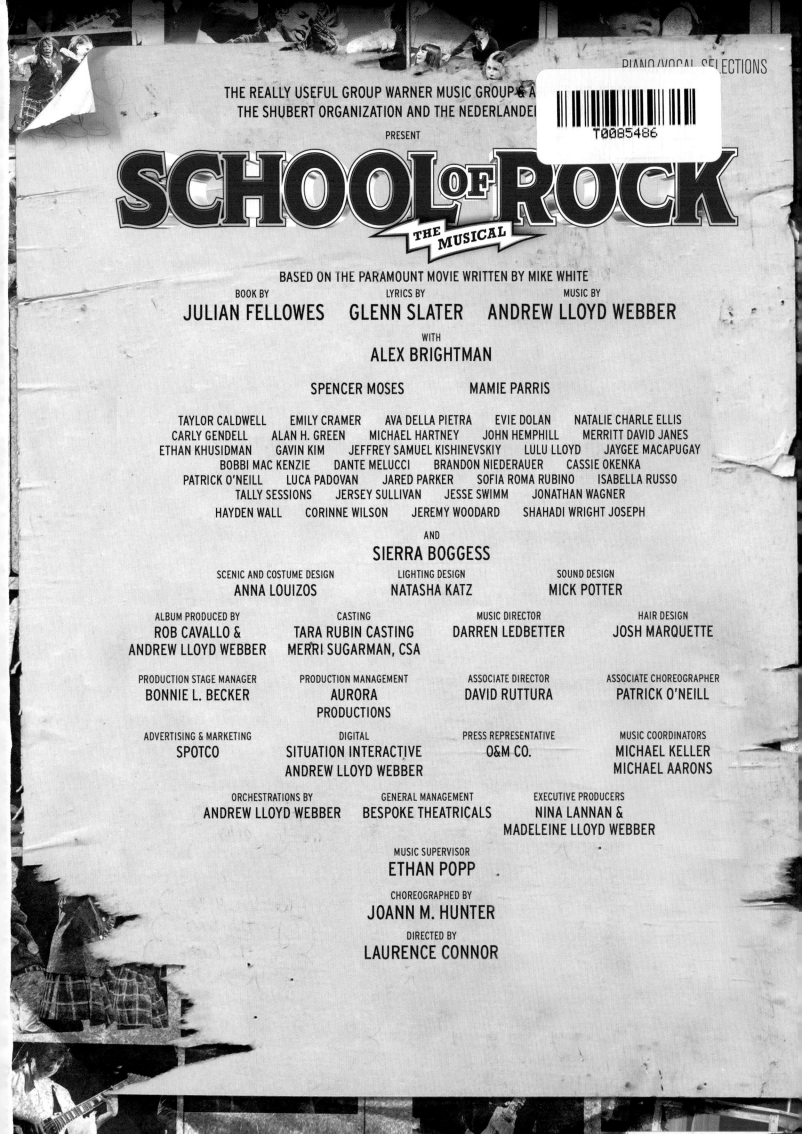

THE REALLY USEFUL GROUP WARNER MUSIC GROUP & A
THE SHUBERT ORGANIZATION AND THE NEDERLANDER

PRESENT

SCHOOL OF ROCK
THE MUSICAL

BASED ON THE PARAMOUNT MOVIE WRITTEN BY MIKE WHITE

BOOK BY	LYRICS BY	MUSIC BY
JULIAN FELLOWES	GLENN SLATER	ANDREW LLOYD WEBBER

WITH

ALEX BRIGHTMAN

SPENCER MOSES   MAMIE PARRIS

TAYLOR CALDWELL   EMILY CRAMER   AVA DELLA PIETRA   EVIE DOLAN   NATALIE CHARLE ELLIS
CARLY GENDELL   ALAN H. GREEN   MICHAEL HARTNEY   JOHN HEMPHILL   MERRITT DAVID JANES
ETHAN KHUSIDMAN   GAVIN KIM   JEFFREY SAMUEL KISHINEVSKIY   LULU LLOYD   JAYGEE MACAPUGAY
BOBBI MAC KENZIE   DANTE MELUCCI   BRANDON NIEDERAUER   CASSIE OKENKA
PATRICK O'NEILL   LUCA PADOVAN   JARED PARKER   SOFIA ROMA RUBINO   ISABELLA RUSSO
TALLY SESSIONS   JERSEY SULLIVAN   JESSE SWIMM   JONATHAN WAGNER
HAYDEN WALL   CORINNE WILSON   JEREMY WOODARD   SHAHADI WRIGHT JOSEPH

AND

SIERRA BOGGESS

SCENIC AND COSTUME DESIGN	LIGHTING DESIGN	SOUND DESIGN
ANNA LOUIZOS	NATASHA KATZ	MICK POTTER

ALBUM PRODUCED BY	CASTING	MUSIC DIRECTOR	HAIR DESIGN
ROB CAVALLO & ANDREW LLOYD WEBBER	TARA RUBIN CASTING MERRI SUGARMAN, CSA	DARREN LEDBETTER	JOSH MARQUETTE

PRODUCTION STAGE MANAGER	PRODUCTION MANAGEMENT	ASSOCIATE DIRECTOR	ASSOCIATE CHOREOGRAPHER
BONNIE L. BECKER	AURORA PRODUCTIONS	DAVID RUTTURA	PATRICK O'NEILL

ADVERTISING & MARKETING	DIGITAL	PRESS REPRESENTATIVE	MUSIC COORDINATORS
SPOTCO	SITUATION INTERACTIVE ANDREW LLOYD WEBBER	O&M CO.	MICHAEL KELLER MICHAEL AARONS

ORCHESTRATIONS BY	GENERAL MANAGEMENT	EXECUTIVE PRODUCERS
ANDREW LLOYD WEBBER	BESPOKE THEATRICALS	NINA LANNAN & MADELEINE LLOYD WEBBER

MUSIC SUPERVISOR
ETHAN POPP

CHOREOGRAPHED BY
JOANN M. HUNTER

DIRECTED BY
LAURENCE CONNOR

Photos by Matthew Murphy & Joan Marcus

SCHOOL OF ROCK
ACCESS ALL AREAS

"School Of Rock" is a story about the empowering force of music. It tells of how music brings joy to people's lives and how it can change people for the better.

Enjoy!

Andrew Ll. Webber

WHEN I CLIMB TO THE TOP OF MOUNT ROCK

Music by ANDREW LLOYD WEBBER
Lyrics by GLENN SLATER

Heavy Rock

DEWEY:
I'll be strum-ming my axe __ in a base-ment dive __ with my to-tal-ly kick-ass band __ when an ar-my of A __ and R men will ar-rive __ with pens and con-tracts in hand. __ And they'll

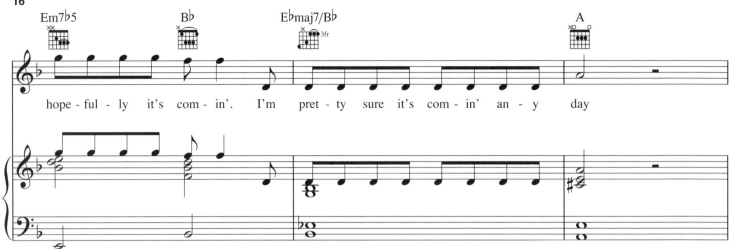

hope - ful - ly it's com - in'. I'm pret - ty sure it's com - in' an - y day

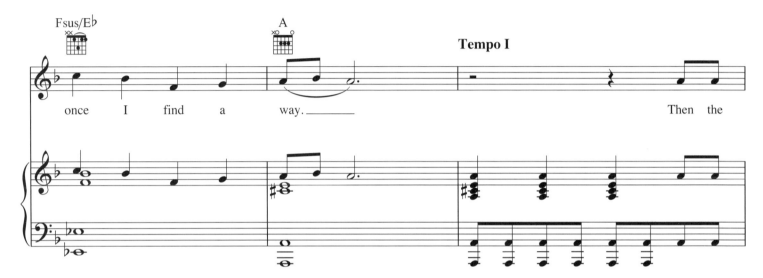

once I find a way._____ Then the

Tempo I

dreams that I've had __ since the day I turned ten __ will be fi - nal - ly com - in' true. _

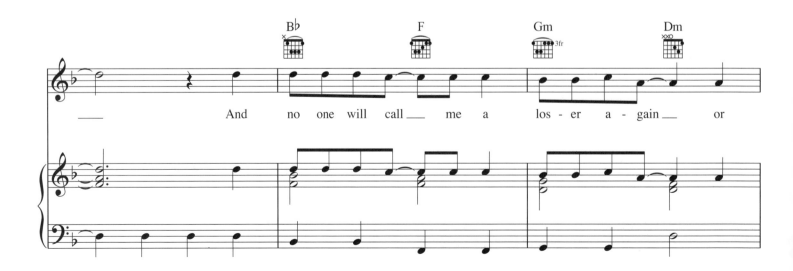

__ And no one will call __ me a los - er a - gain __ or

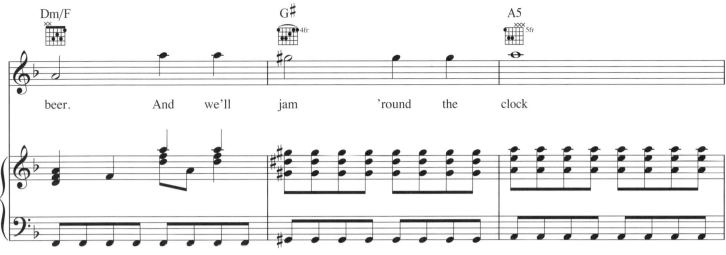

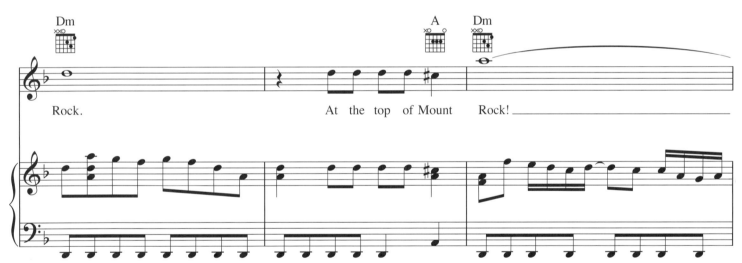

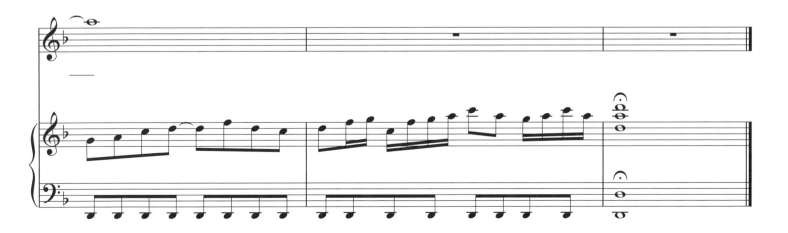

HORACE GREEN ALMA MATER

Music by ANDREW LLOYD WEBBER
Lyrics by GLENN SLATER

KIDS:

Here at Hor - ace Green, we face the fu - ture,
Sol - emn and se - rene, we shoul - der du - ty,

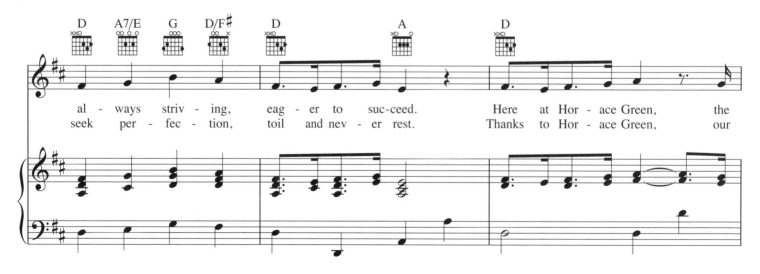

al - ways striv - ing, eag - er to suc - ceed. Here at Hor - ace Green, the
seek per - fec - tion, toil and nev - er rest. Thanks to Hor - ace Green, our

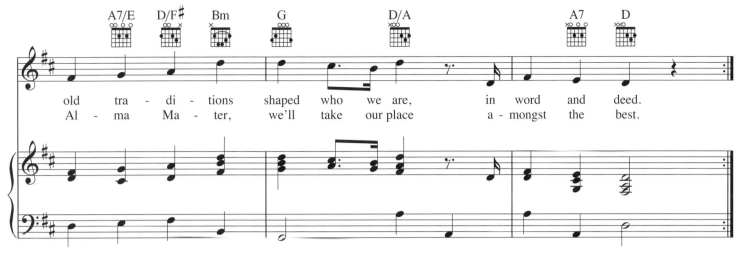

old tra - di - tions shaped who we are, in word and deed.
Al - ma Ma - ter, we'll take our place a - mongst the best.

Military style

add TEACHERS:

Here at Hor - ace Green, we march in lock - step, ev - er up - ward,

Here at Hor - ace Green, we march in lock - step, ev - er up - ward,

des - tined to a - chieve. Here at Hor - ace Green, we go forth proud - ly,

des - tined to a - chieve. Here at Hor - ace Green, we go forth proud - ly,

Des - tined to a - chieve.

HERE AT HORACE GREEN

Music by ANDREW LLOYD WEBBER
Lyrics by GLENN SLATER

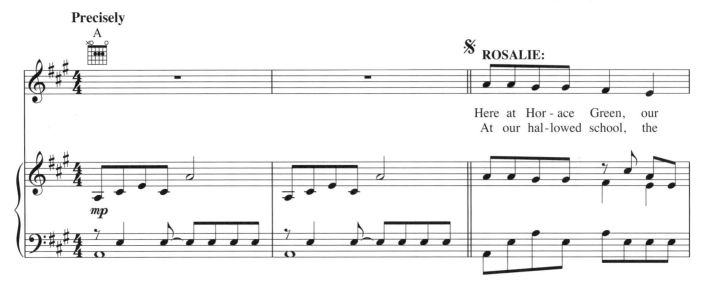

ROSALIE:

Here at Hor - ace Green, our
At our hal - lowed school, the

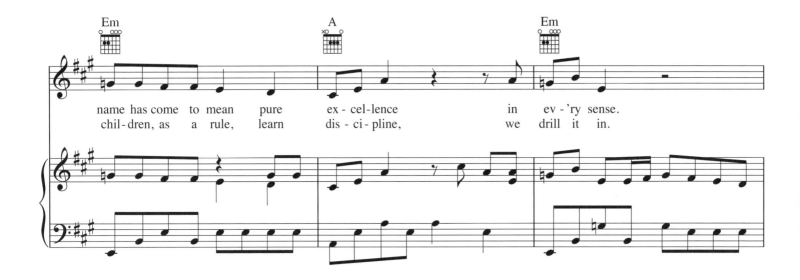

name has come to mean pure ex - cel - lence in ev - 'ry sense.
chil - dren, as a rule, learn dis - ci - pline, we drill it in.

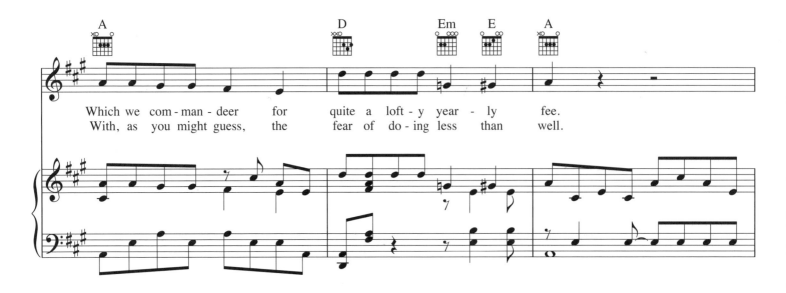

Which we com - man - deer for quite a loft - y year - ly fee.
With, as you might guess, the fear of do - ing less than well.

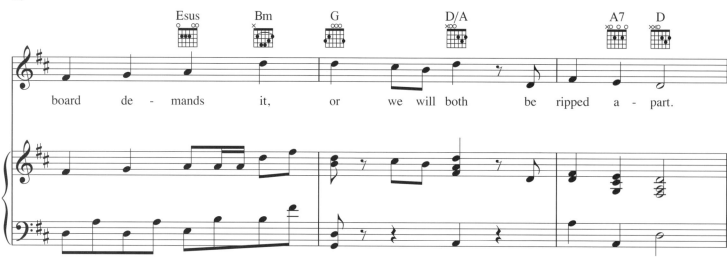

board de - mands it, or we will both be ripped a - part.

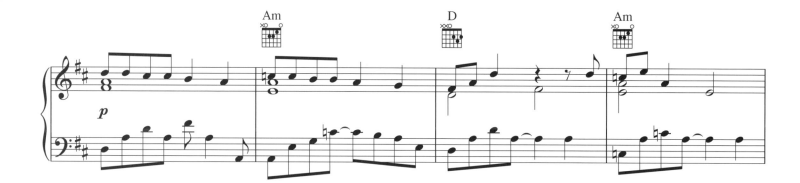

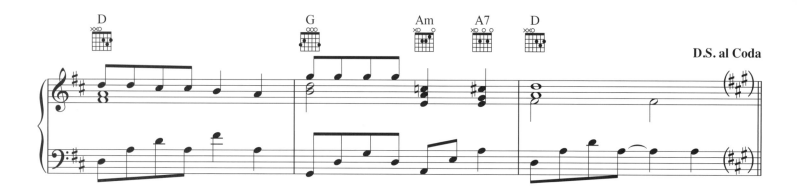

D.S. al Coda

CODA

There's no in be - tween, we get re - sults here. Or the a - lums will hunt us down.

CHILDREN OF ROCK

Music by ANDREW LLOYD WEBBER
Lyrics by GLENN SLATER

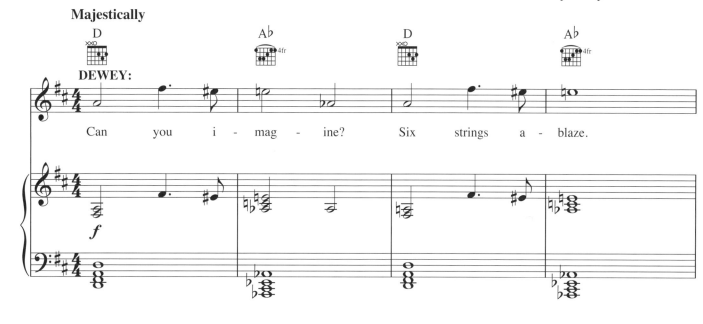

Can you i - mag - ine? Six strings a - blaze.

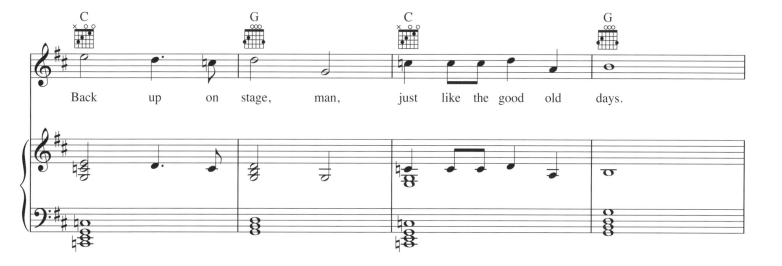

Back up on stage, man, just like the good old days.

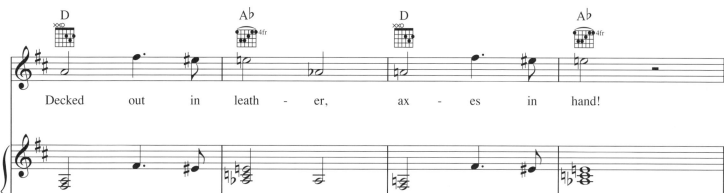

Decked out in leath - er, ax - es in hand!

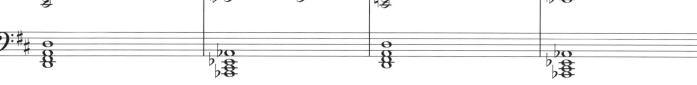

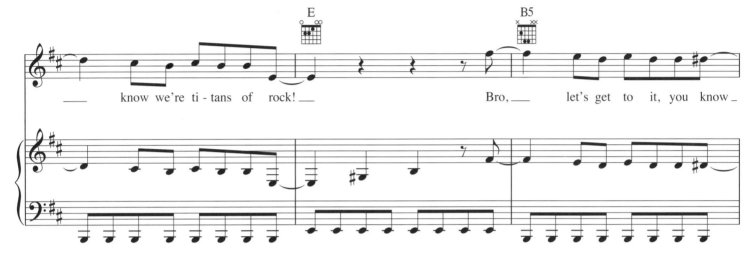

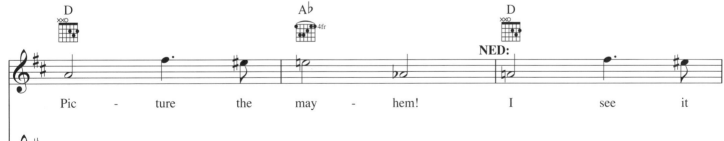

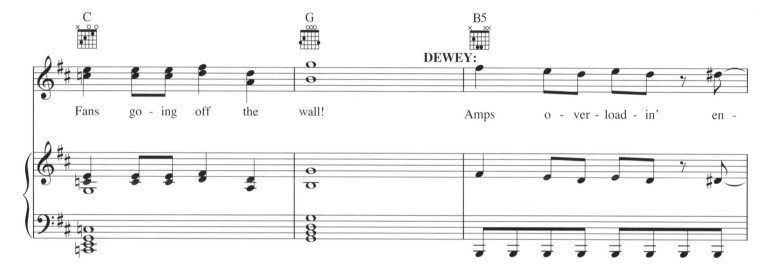

DEWEY: NED:

Rag - ing and reel-ing, Noth - ing like the feel-ing when _

_ you're a Ti - tan of rock! _ Full _ throt-tle jam-min', hard-

BOTH:

- core bod - y slam-min' Death _ Met - al Chil-dren of Rock _

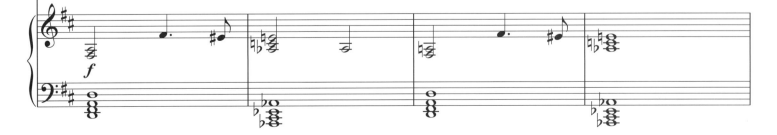

DEWEY: NED:

And when it's o - ver, one migh - ty roar!

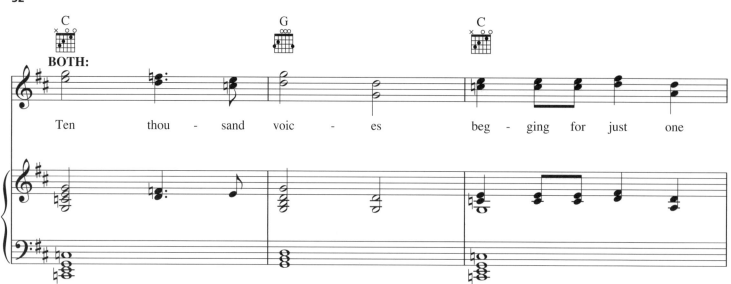

BOTH:

Ten thou - sand voic - es beg - ging for just one

more!

fff

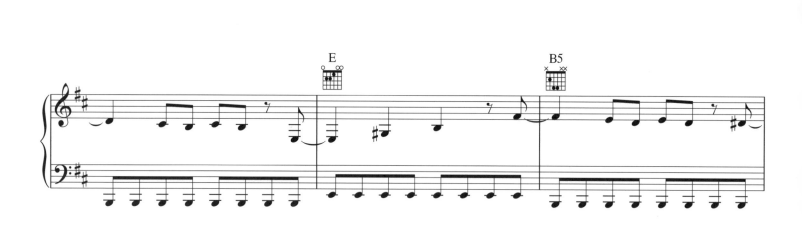

Repeat ad lib.

YOU'RE IN THE BAND

Music by ANDREW LLOYD WEBBER
Lyrics by GLENN SLATER

DEWEY: *Ever play the electric guitar?*
ZACK: *My dad says it's a waste of time.*
DEWEY: *Oh yeah? Well let's waste time together, shall we?*

Grab a hold of your axe ___ and try to pluck out this riff. ___

[DEWEY plucks out a riff on the guitar. ZACK dutifully imitates him.]

Good! Let your shoul-ders re - lax, ___ you don't wan - na be so stiff. ___

[ZACK plays again, with more confidence.] *[ZACK does it one more time, vividly.]*

That's it!

Excellent! Keep on go - in', don't stop, take it o - ver the top. Make each

note real - ly pop, squeeze out ev - 'ry last drop. Give it one fi - nal whop! And

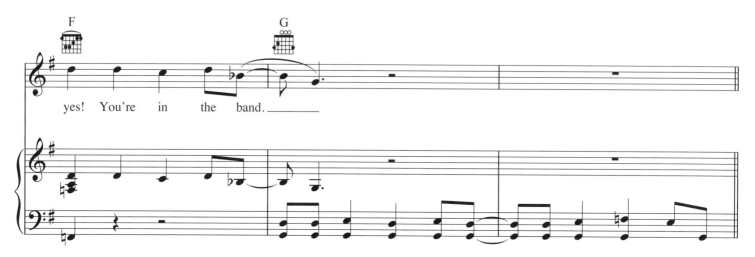

yes! You're in the band._____

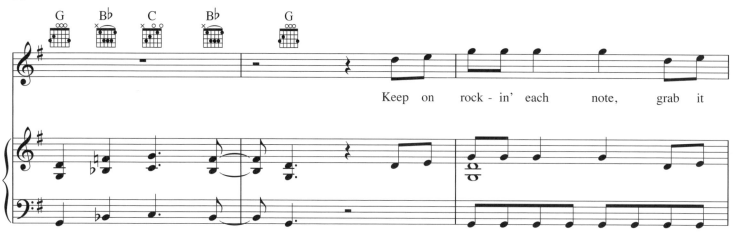

Keep on rock-in' each note, grab it

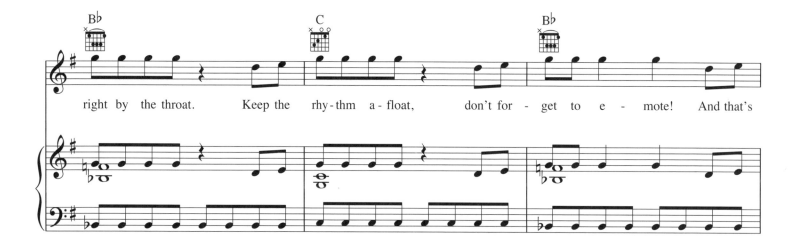

right by the throat. Keep the rhy-thm a-float, don't for-get to e - mote! And that's

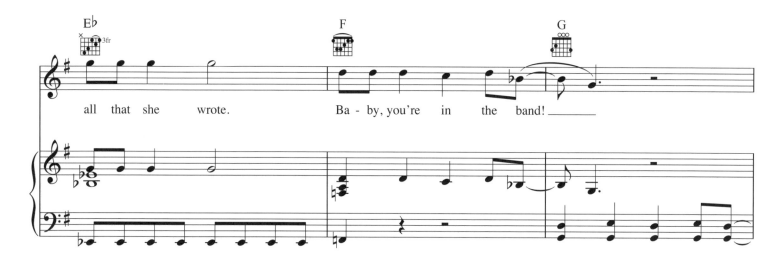

all that she wrote. Ba - by, you're in the band! _____ If you

[Next, he turns to LAWRENCE.]
DEWEY: *Piano man!*
LAWRENCE: *Lawrence.*
DEWEY: *Whatever, dude, come here!*

play the pi - an - o, you can play the keys. ___ **LAWRENCE:** *I only*

play classical. **DEWEY:** So just loos - en it up, and strut your ex - per - tise. __

___ **LAWRENCE:** *I don't think I can.* **DEWEY:** Take a look at this mu - sic and

let your mind ex - pand. __

You're in the band.

DEWEY: *Now who's gonna be my drummer?*
FREDDIE: *I play percussion.*
SUMMER: *You play the cymbals.*
FREDDIE: *Shut up!*
DEWEY: *Shut up!*

DEWEY: *(Last time)*

Sit your butt at the skins __ and try to whack out a beat. _

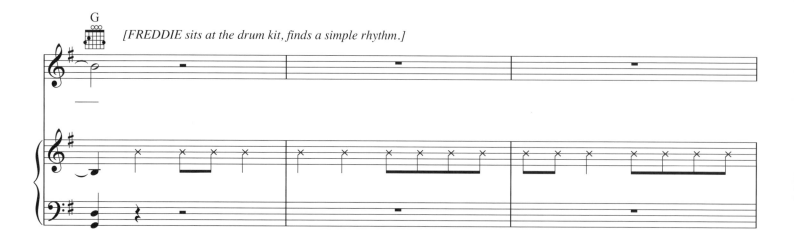

[FREDDIE sits at the drum kit, finds a simple rhythm.]

Not bad. Feel the groove in your pins, ___ then slow-ly turn up the heat. ___

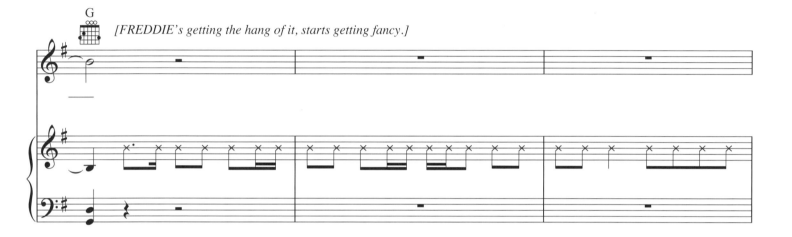

G

[FREDDIE's getting the hang of it, starts getting fancy.]

Bb

And now rat - a - tat - tat. Hit the bass and high hat! Make it

C   Bb   Eb

juic - y and fat! Yeah, ex - act - ly like that! And now shut it down flat...

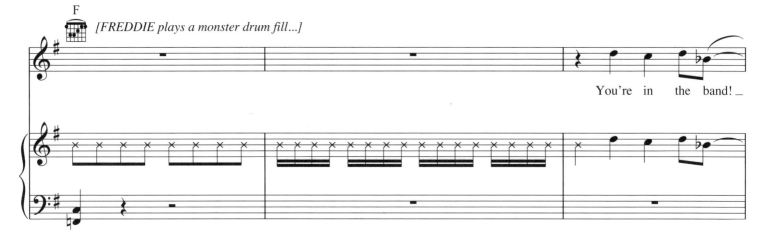

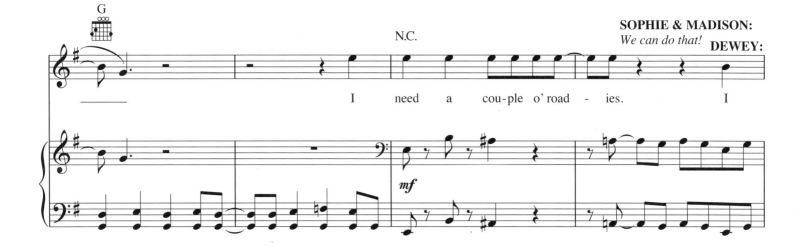

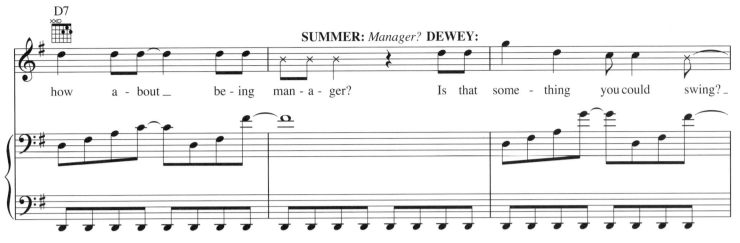

SUMMER: *Manager?* DEWEY:

how a-bout be-ing man-a-ger? Is that some-thing you could swing?

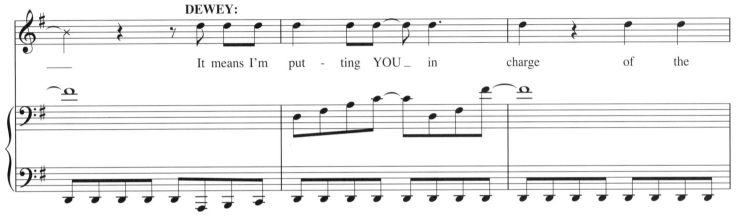

SUMMER: *What does it mean?*

DEWEY:

It means I'm put-ting YOU in charge of the

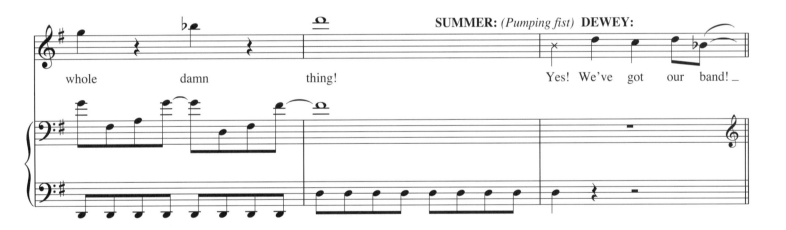

whole damn thing! SUMMER: *(Pumping fist)* DEWEY: Yes! We've got our band!

[All instruments drop out except the drums, played by FREDDIE.]

N.C.

DEWEY *(2nd time)*: Now, Freddie, keep that beat going. Katie, come in on G...

Drums only

Bass (last time only)

DEWEY *(2nd time):* *Just give me that G, lay it down there. Zack, hit me with some big fat chords.*

DEWEY *(2nd time):* *Awesome! Lawrence, take me to the moon!*

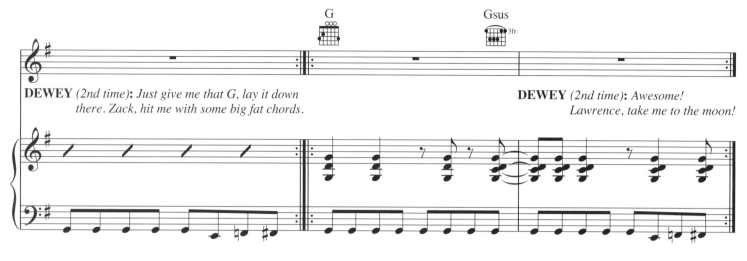

DEWEY: *(Last time)*

Now re - peat af - ter me, ___ "I pledge al -

Ad lib. organ riff

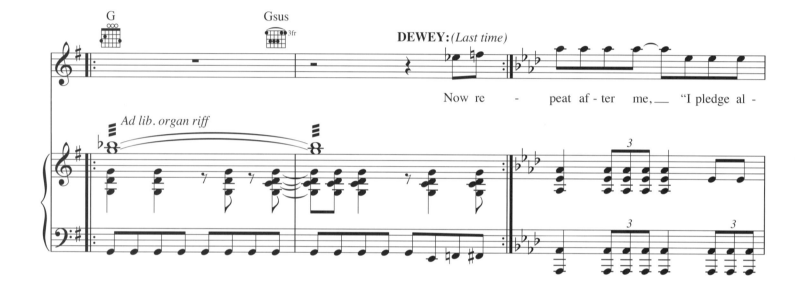

le - giance to the band." ___ "And I

KIDS:

"I pledge al - le - giance to the band." _

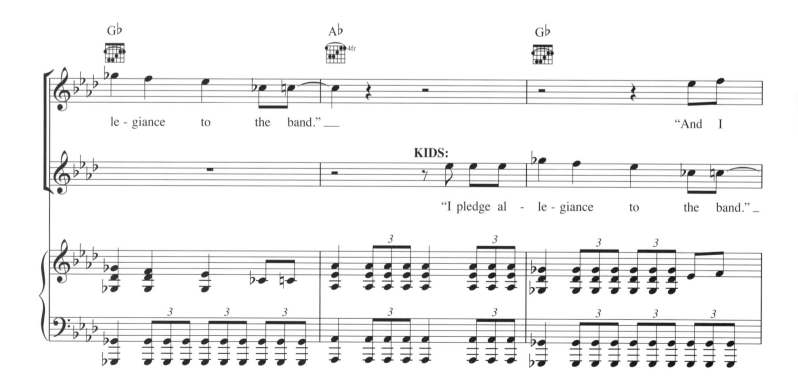

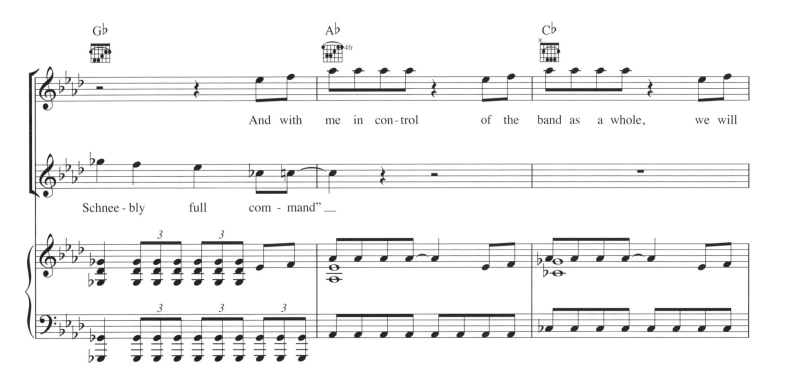

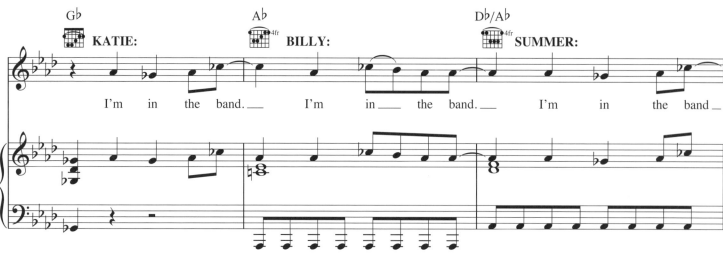

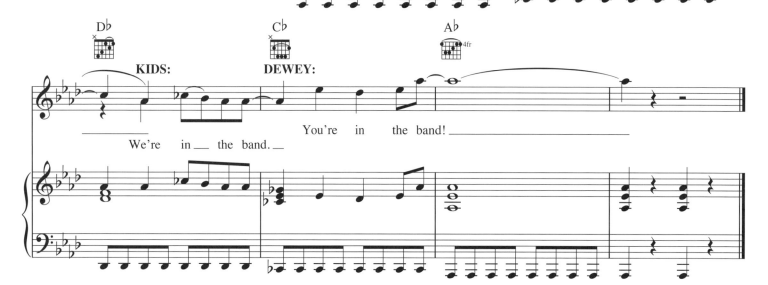

IF ONLY YOU WOULD LISTEN

Music by ANDREW LLOYD WEBBER
Lyrics by GLENN SLATER

Energetic Rock

ZACK: You al-ways talk, talk, talk all the time. ___ You nev-er

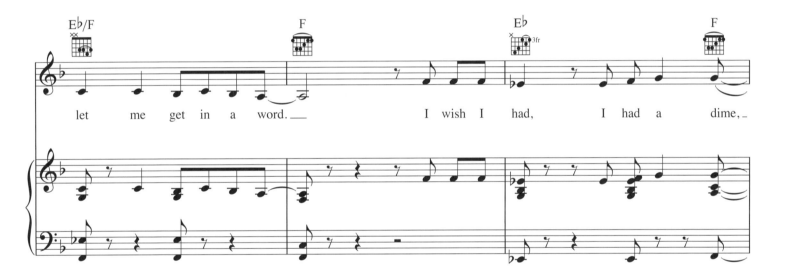

let me get in a word. ___ I wish I had, I had a dime, ___

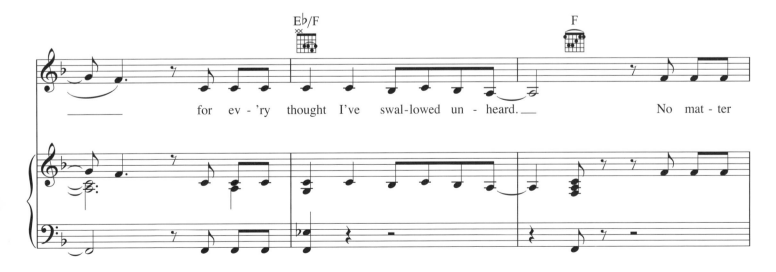

___ for ev-'ry thought I've swal-lowed un-heard. ___ No mat-ter

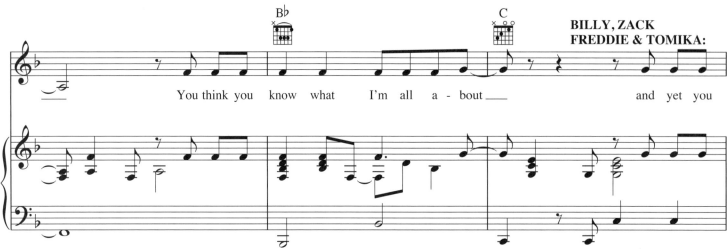

BILLY, ZACK
FREDDIE & TOMIKA:

You think you know what I'm all a-bout ___ and yet you

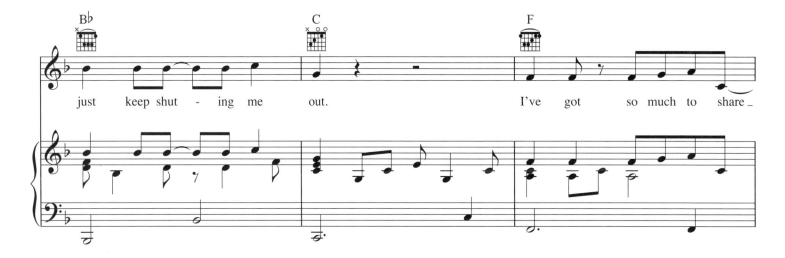

just keep shut - ing me out. I've got so much to share ___

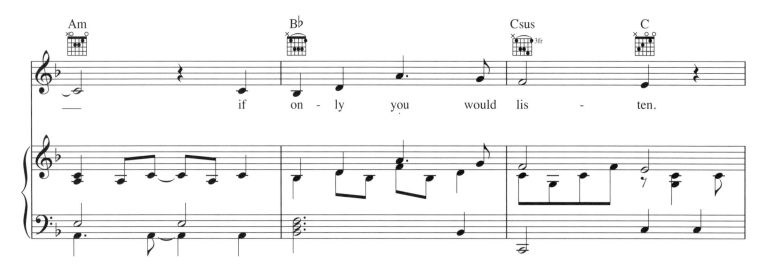

___ if on - ly you would lis - ten.

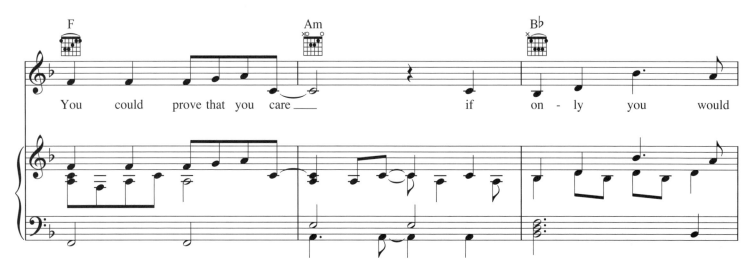

You could prove that you care ___ if on - ly you would

lis - ten. I'm not gon - na beg you, you'll

nev - er see a tear. But, I prom - ise one

LAWRENCE:

day, I'll make you hear. Yeah, you'll see one

MADISON:

day, I'm gon-na make you hear me. Got - ta find a

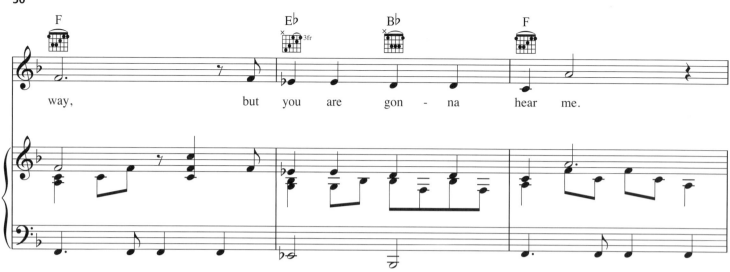

way, but you are gon - na hear me.

MASON & SHONELLE:

Got so much to say and I'm gon - na make you

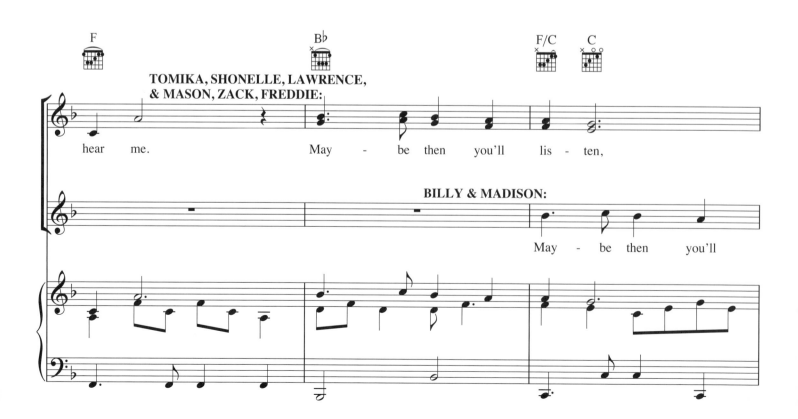

TOMIKA, SHONELLE, LAWRENCE,
& MASON, ZACK, FREDDIE:

hear me. May - be then you'll lis - ten,

BILLY & MADISON:

May - be then you'll

you got - ta lis - ten. You need to
lis - ten, you got - ta lis - ten.

ALL KIDS:
lis - ten, you bet - ter lis - ten!

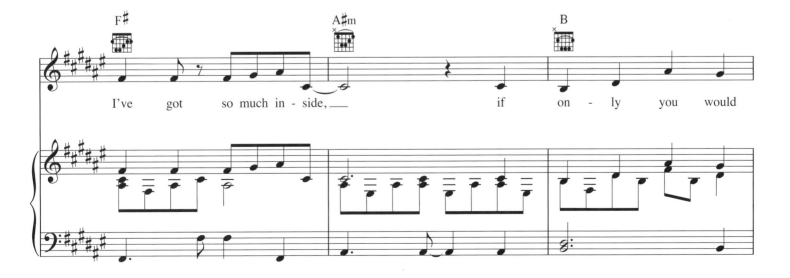

I've got so much in - side, ___ if on - ly you would

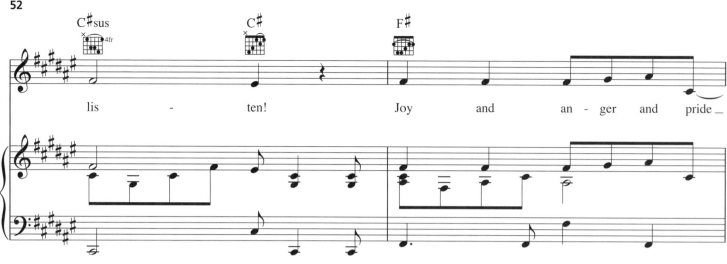

lis - ten! Joy and an-ger and pride ___

___ if on - ly you would lis - ten!

It's not much I'm ask - ing I on - ly want your

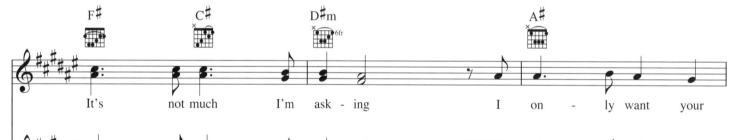

ear. But, I prom-ise one day I'll make you

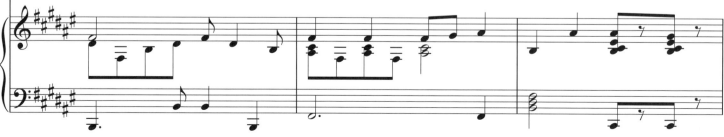

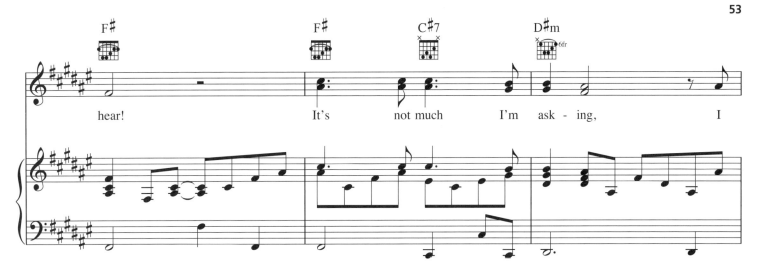

hear! It's not much I'm ask - ing, I

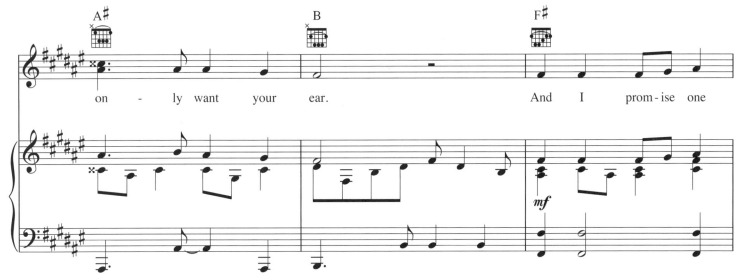

on - ly want your ear. And I prom - ise one

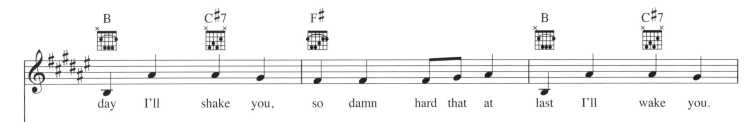

day I'll shake you, so damn hard that at last I'll wake you.

Yeah, I prom - ise one day I'll make you hear!

STICK IT TO THE MAN

Music by ANDREW LLOYD WEBBER
Lyrics by GLENN SLATER

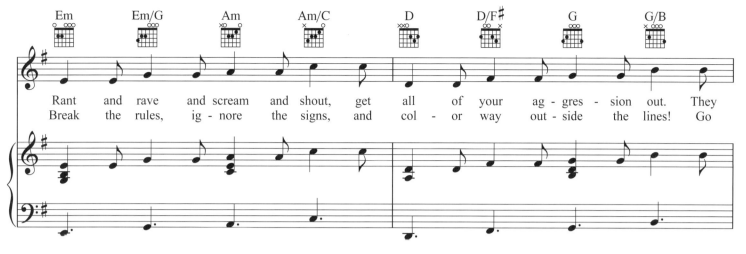

Rant and rave and scream and shout, get all of your ag - gres - sion out. They
Break the rules, ig - nore the signs, and col - or way out - side the lines! Go

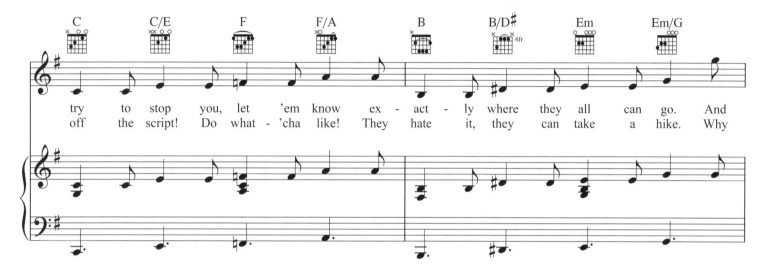

try to stop you, let 'em know ex - act - ly where they all can go. And
off the script! Do what - 'cha like! They hate it, they can take a hike. Why

do it just as loud - ly as you can. Stick it to the man.
live your life to some - one els - e's plan? Stick it to the

man.

TIME TO PLAY

Music by ANDREW LLOYD WEBBER
Lyrics by GLENN SLATER

no de - lays ___ This is for our ré - su - més! ___
act more crude. ___ Bring your best bad at - ti - tude. ___

So it's time to go hard - core.
Band, get rea - dy and let's groove!

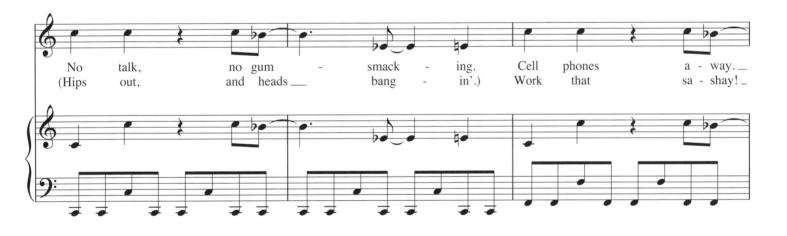

No talk, no gum - smack - ing. Cell phones a - way. ___
(Hips out, and heads ___ bang - in'.) Work that sa - shay! ___

___ Go punk, or start ___ pack - ing
___ Now bring the whole ___ gang ___ in,

Get   to work it's time to play!   Wake   up,   stop day -
Hus - tle up,   it's time to play.   (Hands high,   and fists

- dream - ing. Do   as   I say! _____
_____ pump - ing. Sneers on   dis - play.) _____

Get those   gui - tars _____   scream - ing, Clear   the room, It's
Let's get   this joint _____   jump - ing!   (Bring   it on! It's

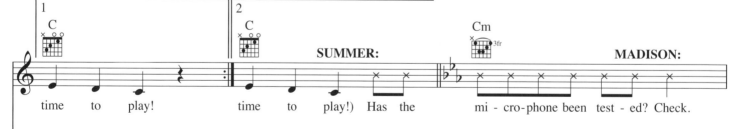

time   to play!   time   to play!) Has the   mi - cro-phone been test - ed? Check.

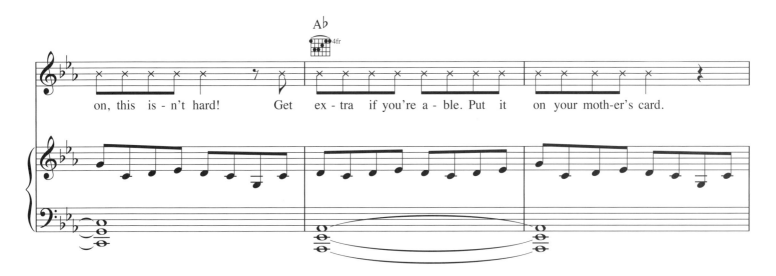

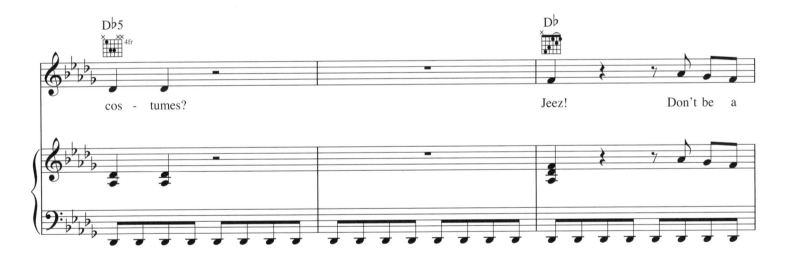

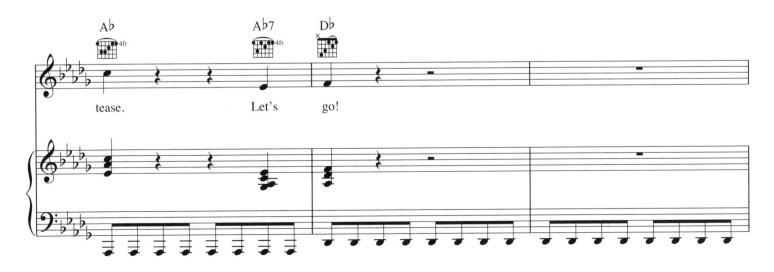

Look, we don't have time to waste _ while you try to

find some taste. _ Fine! Here's the de - sign. Hell

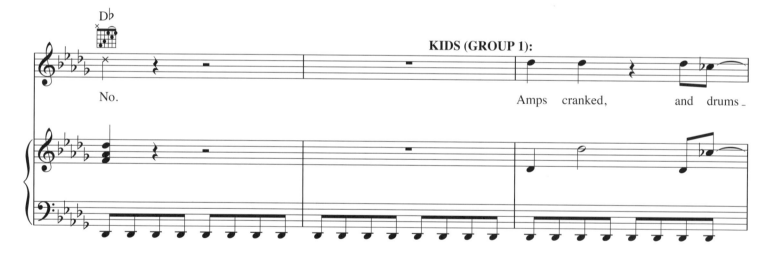

No. Amps cranked, and drums _

_ beat - ing! Don't stop half way! _

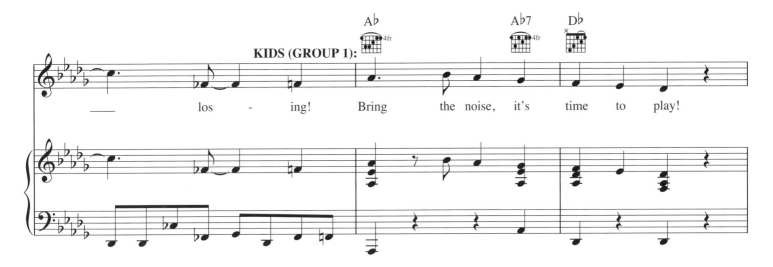

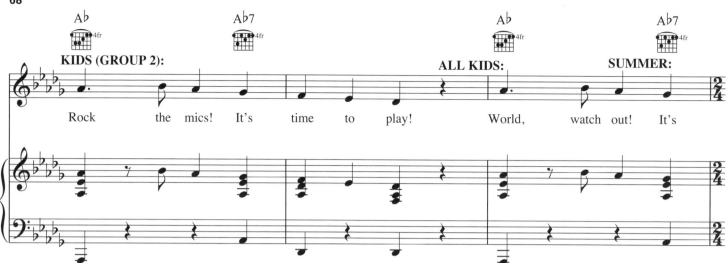

WHERE DID THE ROCK GO?

Music by ANDREW LLOYD WEBBER
Lyrics by GLENN SLATER

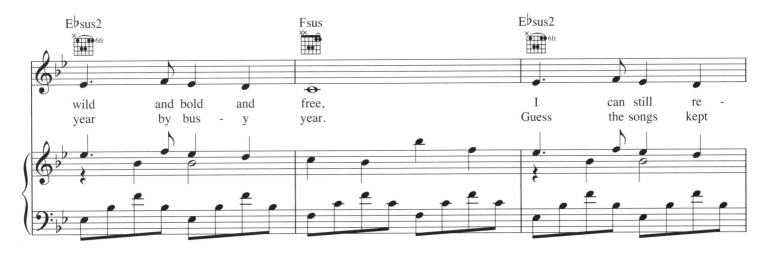

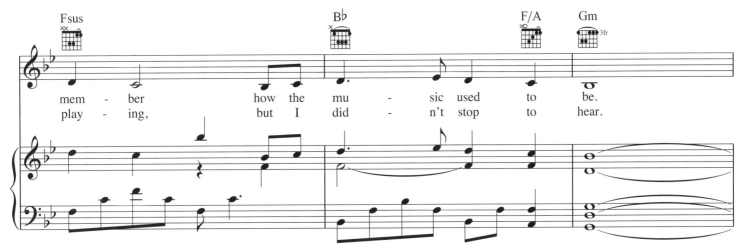

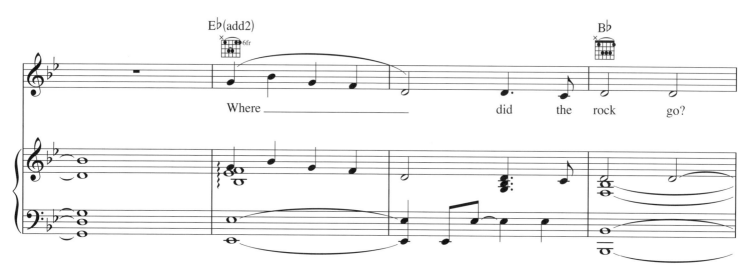

Where's the rat-tle and the roar and the buzz?

Where do last year's one-hit won-ders go to?

And what hap-pened to the girl I was?

D.S. al Coda

CODA

out. Where _____

did the time go? Where's the joy I used to

know way back when? Where's the pow- er and the beau-

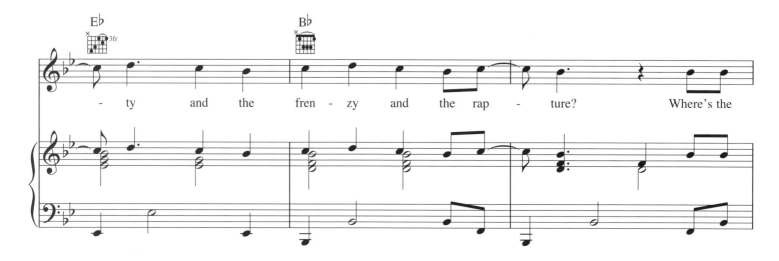

-ty and the fren - zy and the rap - ture? Where's the

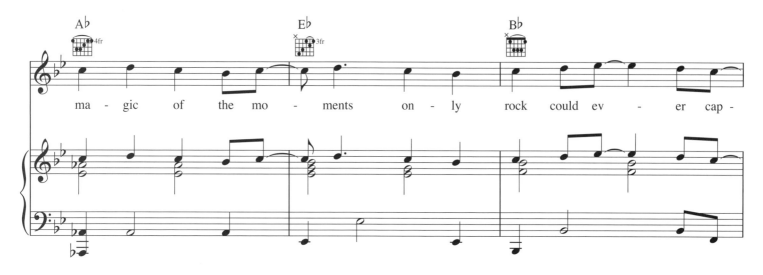

ma - gic of the mo - ments on - ly rock could ev - er cap-

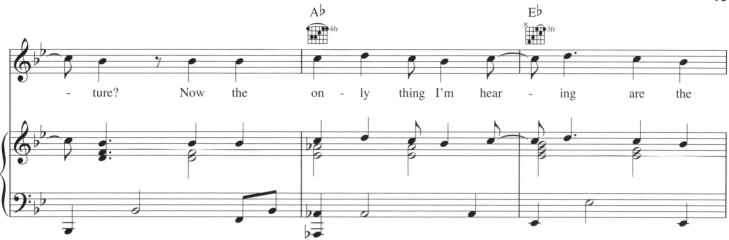

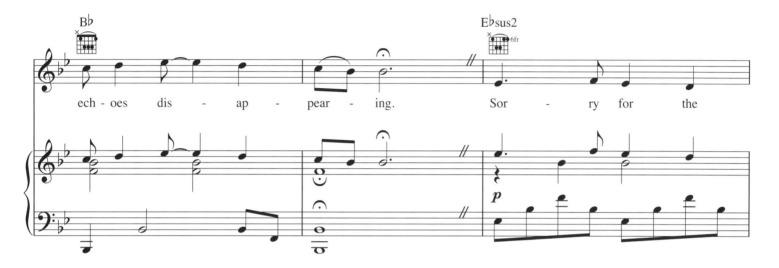

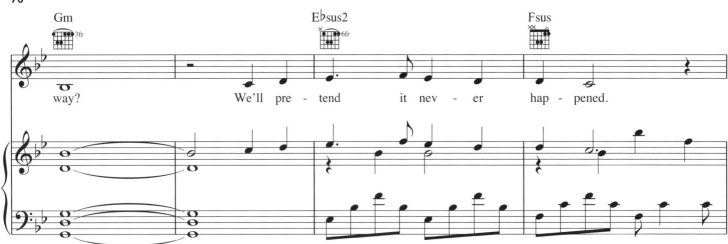

way? We'll pre - tend it nev - er hap - pened.

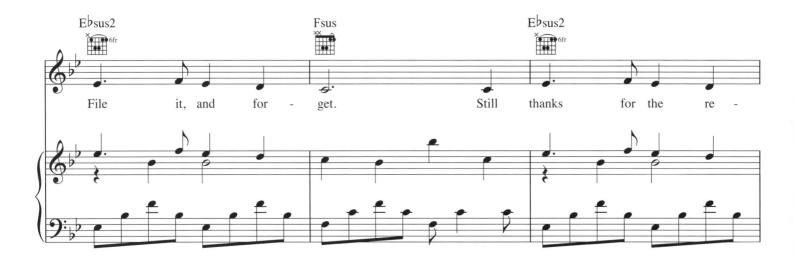

File it, and for - get. Still thanks for the re -

mind - er that there's mu - sic in me yet.

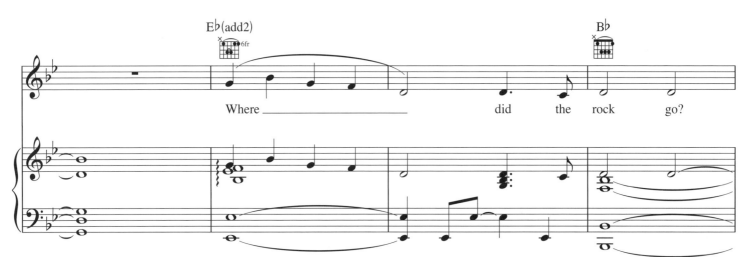

Where _____ did the rock go?

IF ONLY YOU WOULD LISTEN
(Reprise)

Music by ANDREW LLOYD WEBBER
Lyrics by GLENN SLATER

Slow Gospel

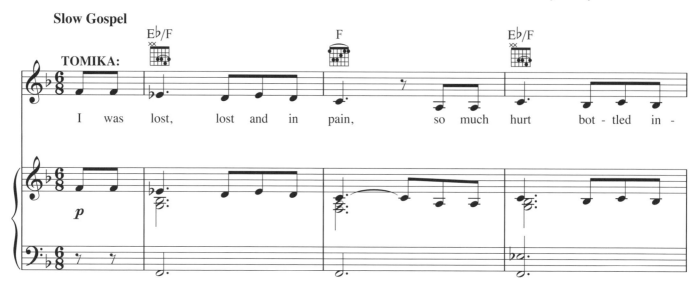

I was lost, lost and in pain, so much hurt bot-tled in-

side. All the things I should've said, I just kept try-ing to hide. And I

thought no-bod-y could. But you... you un-der-stood.

I need-ed to share, and on-ly you would

lis-ten. Hoped some-one would care, and on-ly you would

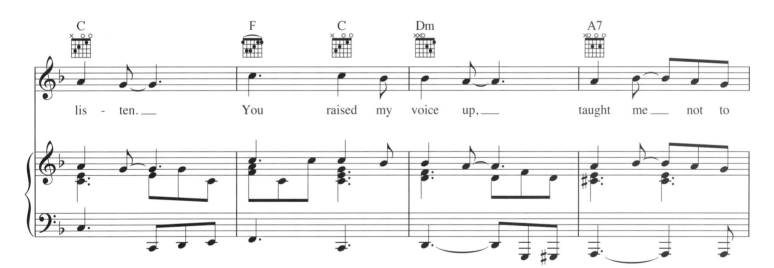

lis-ten. You raised my voice up, taught me not to

fear. I've learned who I am be-cause you're here.

Look a - round. See what you've done? Can't you tell how you came

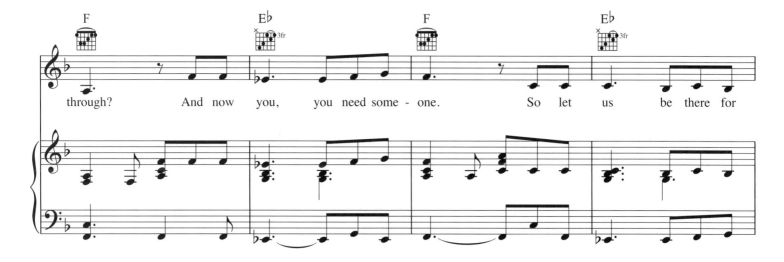

through? And now you, you need some - one. So let us be there for

you. Don't you know we'll un - der - stand be - cause you're, you're in the

ALL KIDS:

band We want you to stay, if

on - ly you would lis - ten! We need you to play, if

on - ly you would lis - ten! __ Now that we've found you, __ you

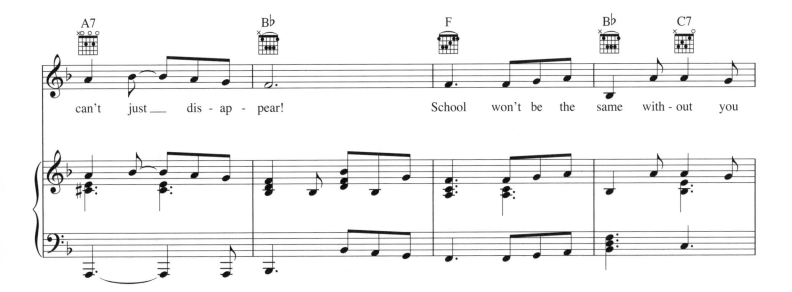

can't just __ dis - ap - pear! School won't be the same with - out you

I'M TOO HOT FOR YOU

Music by ANDREW LLOYD WEBBER
Lyrics by GLENN SLATER

THEO:
Girl, we've been to-geth - er such a-long __ long time. It's been a great three days, you know it's true. But now I can't help think-in' some-thing is-n't right And hon-est-ly, __ it is-n't me, it's

go and lose some weight.   I'm too hot for you

Ha - ha that's mean!

Aah

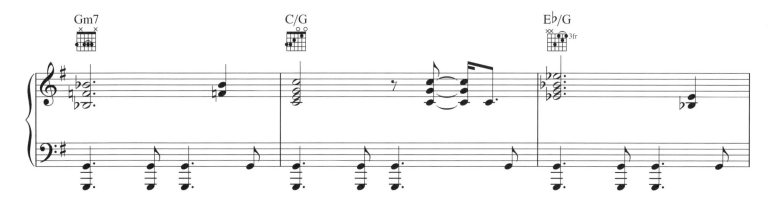

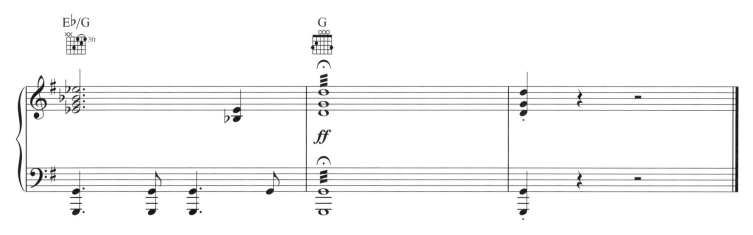

SCHOOL OF ROCK

Words and Music by MIKE WHITE
and SAMUEL BUONAUGURIO

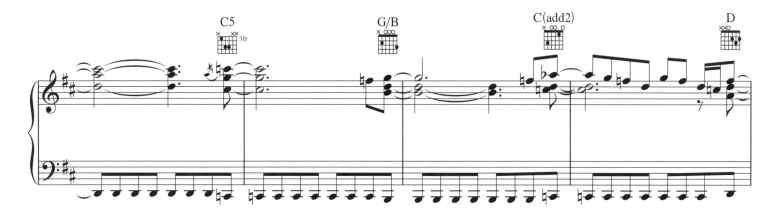

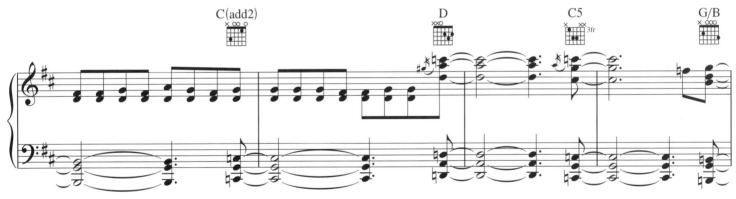

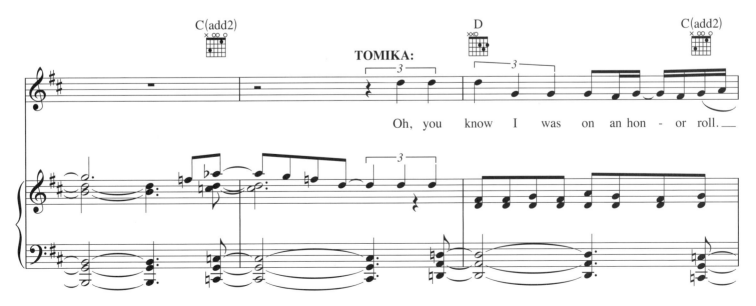

rock got no rhyme._ You bet-ter get me to school_ on time..._

___ la la la Ooh _____

sfz *cresc.*

All right!

f

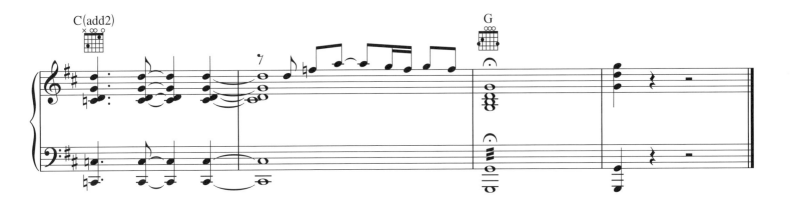